Brijnanda

{50 Selected poetry on Radhey Krishna in Hindi with English meanings}

Bhavini Singh

Content

45. **Radhey stays, Radhey heals**
46. **His infinite love**
47. **His smile**
48. **When Krishna becomes your first and last priority**
49. **My tears are only wept my Kanha**
50. **His beauty**

- **Meera Bai (not a woman but an ocean full of love and devotion)**

A word with author

I Bhavini, a teenager from Uttarakhand and the author of the book Brijnanda (50 selected poetry on Radhey Krishna), though this book my main moto is to spread love and awareness about Krishna Bhakti, yes being a teenager engaging in Krishn Bhakti is one of my biggest achievement ! For you all, it might be a joke, but my dear at the tender age of 8 ! I surrendered myself towards my Damodar, each and every thing which I had prayed, had always got and though poetry which just I had contributed all that to my Kanaha. Well, I can't express my love and devotion in words.

But I am sure glad that the reader, who will be reading these poetries sure be thinking about my Lord. Because each and every Shayri is been written by bottom of my heart. Well to say at this early age engaging in devotion is what my soul wanted just for inner peace which I couldn't found that on rushing world. The sacred love and inner peace which I could get is under my Krishna 's and Radha's lotus feet!

Radhey Radhe

Acknowledgement

Well, to say this book would be a little contribution from my side to my Shree Dhara Madhava's and Shree Mati's lotus feet. There are so many people in this world but some of them are so special for me, we'll I would like to thanks all of them and in particular:

MR. ANAND KUMAR SINGH - My father, who always taught me to be independent and for you it doesn't matter that who thinks about you or not.

MRS. ASHA BAJPAI- My Guru, and a great teacher of my life and because of her only today at this teenage I stepped into the world of authors. She is also a poetess and an author, and she encouraged me to express my feelings in poetries.

MRS. ANCHAL ARORA – A great mentor more than an English teacher! She was one of the only one who had taught me to visualize and to decide the correct path!

Well, we can say that some special people are just made for some other special person! And at last, but not the least, my lord Jagannath who always stayed with me at every time. He is my first and a last priority.

Radhey Govinda

1

Once upon a Meera....

मुझको नहीं रहना इस कलयुग में कान्हा,
गिर गई हु गलती से इस संसार में।

हर दिन तुझको याद कुरु मैं, अपनी आँखों के दीदार से.

याद है वो दिन मेरे को जब मैं हारी , फिर तेरी भक्ति मे आकार में अपनी पूरी दुनिया वारी।

तू मेरा प्यार और मेरा परिवार, वादा कर तू हर पल रहेगा मेरे साथ जब भी होगा मुझपे वार।

कान्हा! लोग तो बस घुर कर चले जाते हैं, मेरे मुरलीधर हम तो बस तुम्हें चाहते हैं।

हार गयी थी मैं तो तूने अपनाया है, उंगली पकड़ कर चलाना सिखाया है।

कलयुग में राधा रानी तो सब बनना चाहते हैं, लेकिन कोई माँ सीता बनना नहीं चाहता।

हे कृष्ण! गोपी सब बनना चाहते हैं, पर कोई तुम्हारी मीरा नहीं बनना चाहता।

पता नहीं कैसे लगी तुम्हारी लत मुझको?

मेरे कान्हा तेरा अहसान तो कभी भूल नहीं सकती,

पता है कि तू मेरे खून के रिश्ते में नहीं है,

देने को सिर्फ दिल दे सकती हूं तुझको।

बस आखिरी में ये कहना चाहती हूँ, भलेही पूरी नहीं पर मैं तेरी मीरा बन जाती हूं।

बस एक वादा कर मुझसे, मुझे समा लेना दिल से अपने।

Meaning :-

I don't want to live in this Kalyug Kanha, I have fallen into this world by mistake.

I remember you every day, through my eyes.

I remember that day when I was defeated , then your devotion transformed my entire world into my shape.

You are my love and my family, promise me that you will be with me every moment, whenever I am attacked.

Krishna! People just stare and go away, my Murlidhar, we just love you.

When I was defeated, you accepted me and taught me to walk by holding my finger.

In Kalyug, everyone wants to become Radha Rani, but no one wants to become Mata Sita.

Hey Krishna! Everyone wants to be Gopi, but no one wants to be your Meera.

I don't know how I got addicted to you?

My Kanha, I can never forget your favor.

I know that you are not my blood relation,

I can only give you my heart to give.

I just want to say this in the end, even if not completely, I will become your Meera.

Just make a promise to me, take me with your heart.

2

Gopi Vallabh....

कोने पे बैठी यमुना किनारे, गोपी जाने किसको निहारे?

हमरो है वो नंद के दुलारे, गोपी वल्लभ कृष्ण हमारे.

Meaning :-

Sitting on the corner, on the banks of Yamuna, Gopi knows whom to look at?

He is of our beloved Nand, Gopi Vallabh Krishna is ours.

3

When Kanha becomes your happiness....

कान्हा कान्हा हर पल पुकारु, तेरे तस्वीर को यु मैं निहारु।

तेरी बाते मेरे मन को भाते, मेरे मनमोहक वो कृष्ण कहलाते।

Meaning:-

I call Kanha Kanha every moment, I gaze at your beauty.Your words are pleasing to my mind, he is my favorite and is called Krishna.

4

My past life....

वो दिन भी क्या दिन था मेरा,

जब इस दुनिया से मैंने धोखा खाया।

सिर्फ कान्हा साथ था मेरा,

जब इस दुनिया से इतनी ठोकरें खायी।

Meaning:-

What a day that day was for me,

When I felt betrayed by this world.

Only Kanha was with me,

When I lost so much from this world.

5

Krishn Bhakti....

फिर शरण मिली जो तेरी आई,

यू जो तूने मेरी जिंदगी सजाई .

सारे कष्ट तेरे दरबार मे आकर गाई,

हे कृष्ण! कभी मे उसे भुला ना पायी ।

Meaning:-

Then I got the refuge that came from you,

You who decorated my life.

All the troubles come and but still I sang in your court,

Hey Krishna! I would never forget that everlasting momery.

6

Shree Radhey....

श्री राधा राधा नाम रट्टू मैं,

हर पल तेरा ध्यान करुं।

मेरे दिल में बस एक ही नाम है,

मेरे श्री राधे श्याम.

Meaning :-

Shri Radha Radha is use to speak,

I use to meditate on you every moment.There is only one name in my heart,My Shri Radhe Shyam.

7

My love for Krishna....

मेरा प्यार तेरे लिए सागर से गहरा,

शायद तुझे एहसास है जो मेरा दिल कह रहा।

मेरा प्यार तेरे लिए है कुछ ऐसा,

पता है कि मैं ढूँढ़ न पाऊंगी कोई तेरे जैसा ।

Meaning:-

My love for you is deeper than the ocean,

Maybe you realize what my heart is saying.

My love for you is something like this,

I know that I will never find someone like you.

8

Oh Krishna! Call me to your palace....

प्रभु मुझे बुलालो अपने धाम,

मुझे नहीं बिताना यहाँ दिन और शाम

इस दुनिया में कोई अब मेरा ना है,

हे कृष्ण! तू ही अब मेरा सहारा रहा.

Meaning:-

Lord, call me to your abode,

I don't want to spend my days and evenings here

No one is mine in this world anymore,

Hey Krishna! You are only my support now.

9

My Leeladhar....

फूल चढ़ावत, गीतम गावत,

मेरे कान्हा माखन खावत.

लीला उनकी अपरम्पार ,

है वो मेरो नन्द के लाल।

Meaning :-

Flower offering, Geetam Gavat,

My Kanha eats butter.His leela is unconventional, He is nand's boy.

10

Letter to Krishna....

हे कान्हा! जो तेरे सच्चे द्वार में आता है,

यू खाली हाथ कभी ना जाता है.

तेरी एक झलक के लिए तड़प उठे है तेरे सारे भक्त,

हे कान्हा! कैसे भेजूँ अपना मैं ये खत?

Meaning :-

Hey Kanaha! Who comes to your true court,

Never goes empty handed.

All your devotees are yearning for a glimpse of you,

Hey Kanha! How can I express my feelings to you?

11

Waiting for him....

कैसे भेजु खत ,

करती मैं कई बार बातें।

आँखें मेरी करती है,

टुकुर - टुकुर दिन-रातें।

मेरे कृष्ण का इंतज़ार,

अब मुझसे ना हो पाता.

ओ नन्द के लाल,

इस कलयुग में दर्शन तो दे जाता!

Meaning :-

How should I send the message,

I talks many times.

My eyes do,

Too many days and nights.

Waiting for my Krishna,

Now I don't know.

O son of Nand,

You Would have given darshan in this Kalyug!

12

When krishna becomes your everything....

मेरी हर सांस में तेरा ही वास,

मेरी हर एहसास में तेरा ही नाम.

मेरे हर काम में तेरा ही शान,

हे कृष्ण! तू ही मेरा एक वरदान.

Menaing :-

You reside in my every breath,

Your name is in every feeling of mine.

Your pride is in all my work,Hey Krishna!

You are only my precious blessing.

13

For his Arrival....

कितने दिनों से बैठी हूँ इस चौखट पर,

सिर्फ तेरे इंतजार में।

हर पल तेरा नाम रटूँ मैं,

सिर्फ एक इत्तफाक में।

Meaning :-

For how many days have I been sitting on this bench?

Just waiting for you.

Every moment your name is in my heart, Just a coincidence.

14

Mere Giridhar, Mere Muralidhar....

गिरि को धरण, मेरे गिरिधर।

मुरली बजावत, मेरे मुरलीधर।

चाँद के जैसे मेरे श्याम,

हे कान्हा! मैं आई तेरे धाम.

Meaning :-

Hold on to the mountain, my Giridhar. Murali Bajawat, my Murlidhar.

My Shyam is like the moon, Hey Kanha! I have come to your place.

15

Chanting Radhey....

बरसाने वाली राधा रानी,

दे-दे शरण मुझे तिहारी।

हर पल मुझे तेरी याद सताती,

श्री राधे राधे जब मैं गाती.

Meaning :-

Radha Rani who is Barsaney wali

Give me shelter Tihari.

I miss you every moment,

Shri Radhe Radhe when I chant.

16

Miracle do happen with Krishna....

मैं बावरिया जो तुझे समज न पायी ,

तेरे आने से पहले मेरी आत्मा इतनी दुःख खायी।

इस दुनिया के रीत में,

यू पता नहीं मैं तेरे हाथ थामे मुस्कुराई!

Meaning :-

I Bavaria which you could not understand,

My soul suffered so much before you came.

In the manner of this world,

This even don't know why I smiled holding your hand.

17

Either because of my luck or Karma, I got Damodar....

ना जाने कान्हा कैसे मिले तुम मुझको?

और मेरी भक्ति ने कैसे बांध लिया तुझको?

हे कान्हा! मुझसे कभी रूठियो मत,

पहले से ही टूटी हुई हूं दामोदर, मुझे कभी भूलियो मत।

Menaing :-

Don't know Kanha, how did you meet me?

And how did my devotion had tighten you?

Hey Kanha! Don't ever get angry with me,

I am already broken Damodar, don't ever leave me.

18

Everything is in his lotus feet....

मेरा आने वाला कल तो तुम्हारे हाथो में है,

हे मेरे दामोदर! मेरा बीता हुआ कल तो

तुम्हारी यादों में है!

Meaning :-

My future is in your hands,

Oh my Damodar! My past is in your memories!

19

Govind's Meera....

गोविंद तेरी बंसी सुनि मीरा यूं दौड़ी,

तेरे द्वार पे बैठी मीरा यूं तेरी बंसी सुन के कैसे खोई .

Meaning :-

Govind, after listening to your flute, Meera ran away.

Mira, sitting at your door and listen to your flute.

Look how beautifully she is remembering you ?

20

Krishna Heals, Krishna Stays....

उनकी आंखें मेरी हर पीड़ा समझती,

उनके चाले यू मेरा मन पुलकित करती।

मेरे कृष्ण, मेरी हर इच्छा से बढ़ कर,

क्योंकि उनकी रूह - रूह मेरा हर दर्द समझती ।

Meaning: -

His eyes understood my every pain,

His walk makes my heart happy.

My Krishna, greater than all my desires,

Because his soul understood my every pain.

21

Oh! Krishna let me get one chance....

हे दामोदर! आप मुझे अपनी फूलो जैसी चरण में शरण दे दीजिए,

हे कान्हा! मुझे आप अपनी मुस्कुराहट की एक वजह बनने दीजिए।

Meaning :-

Hey Damodar! Please give me shelter at your flower-like feet.

Hey Kanha! Let me be the reason for your smile.

22

Krishn do returns.....

कुछ लोग कहते हैं कि अगर कोई लौट जाता है तो कभी वापस नहीं आता,

अगर ऐसा ही होता तो, मेरे कान्हा फिर हर गोपी के सपने में क्यों आता?

Meaning :-

Some people say that if someone goes back he never comes back,

If it was like this, then why would my Kanha come in the dreams of every Gopi?

23

When Krishna becomes your whole world....

यू जो तुमने अपना हाथ मेरे सिर पे रखा,

तो मानो मैंने पूरी दुनिया जीत ली हो।

दुनिया की हर वो चीज मुझे मिल गई कान्हा

जब मैंने तेरे तस्वीर को देखा.

Meaning:-

You who placed your hand on my head,

So as if I have conquered the whole world.

I have got everything in the world,

When I saw your picture.

24

Barsaney wali....

श्री राधे आप कब बरसाएंगे अपना आशीर्वाद मुझ पे?

दिन रात करती हूं ये बात ख़ुद से।

कहते हैं जब आप आएंगे तब मेरे कान्हा भी आएंगे ना,

मान लो कभी उनको मेरी याद आ गई, तो जब भी वो आएंगे तो कभी छोड़ के तो नहीं जाएंगे ना!

Meaning :-

Shri Radhe, when will you shower your blessings on me?

I talk to myself about this all day and night.

It is said that when you will come then only my Kanha will also come, right?

Whenever , if he will remembers me, then whenever he comes, he will never ever leave me alone like this, right?

25

Radhey Shyam....

गोविंद गोपाल यदुवंशी,

बांकेबिहारी तू सुन ले मेरी.

Menaing :-

Govind Gopal Yaduvanshi,

Banke Bihari, please listen to me.

26

Hear me Gopal....

मोर मुकुट है सिर पे धारण ,

चंचल उसकी चाल है.

मीरा के प्रभु गिरीधारनागर ,

राधा के वो श्याम है.

Meaning :-

Peacock crown is on the head,

Playful is his way.Mira's Lord Giridharnagar,

He is Shyam of Radha.

27

The devotes love to dance in his Dhun....

हमें तो उनकी धुन में नाचने की आदत है,

हम भक्ति के लिए हैं तो हमारे राधे वल्लभ ही हमारी अमानत हैं।

Meaning :-

We have a habit of dancing in his's tune,

If we are for devotion then our Radhe Vallabh is our trust.

28

Shree Dhara Madhava....

गोपी मनोहर राधे वल्लभा,

जयते जयते श्री धरा माधवा!

Meaning :-

Gopi Manohar Radhe Vallabha,

Jayate Jayate Shri Dhara Madhva!

29

My talk to Krishna....

तो फिर मैंने अपने कान्हा से कहा -

हे कान्हा! अब नहीं खाने मुझे इतने धोखे,

आखिर जिन पर मुझे भरोसा है वो ही क्यों देते हैं मुझे इतनी ठोकरें?

Meaning :-

Then I said to my Kanha –

Hey Kanha! Now I don't want to be deceived so much,

After all, why do the people I trust give me so much slack?

30

Krishna is the supreme creator and controller....

क्या करनी, क्या भरनी

आखिर मैं सब कृष्ण में ही समानी।

दुख - सुख में तू रट ले नाम,

राधे-राधे जय श्री श्याम।

Meaning :-

What to do, what to leave.

After all, everything is going to merge in to Krishna.

You should try to memorize the name in sorrow and happiness,

Radhe-Radhe Jai Shri Shyam.

31

Krishna always help....

जब-जब मैं हारी हूँ कान्हा,

हर पल तुझे निहारी हूँ।

तू अकेला यूं मेरा हाथ थामा,

हर पल मेरा साथ थामा.

मैं बावरिया जो तुझे समाज न पायी,

इस जग की रीत में अपना भला समझ न पायी.

Meaning :-

Whenever I am failed Kanha,

I look at you every moment.

You are alone, you held my hand,

Be with me every moment.

I Bavaria, which did not find my
own standard in society,

I even don't understanded my own
status in this society.

32

His eyes!....

हे कान्हा! अपने ये दयालु नयन,

कभी मुझ पे बरसा देना.

अगर कभी मेरी याद आए तो,

एक बार दामोदर अपने दर्शन दे जाना।

Meaning :-

Hey Kanha! These kind eyes of yours,Shower on me sometime.

If you ever remember me,Damodar should give his darshan once.

33

A normal day of Vrindavan....

वृन्दावन में धेनु चलावे,

माखन चोरी कर के खाये.

नटखट कितनी धूम मचावे,

बंसी की धुन पे सबको नचावे.

Meaning :-

Let the cows run in Vrindavan,

Eat butter by stealing it.

How much noise this kanha makes? Make everyone dance on the tune of his flute.

34

Krishna is everything....

यूं मीरा के ख्यालों में कृष्ण,

राधा के सास - सास में कृष्ण,

गोपियों की खुशियाँ में कृष्ण,

यूं पल - पल मे कृष्ण,

दुनिया के हर कोने में कृष्ण.

Meaning :-

Krishna in Meera's thoughts,

Krishna in Radha's breath,

The happiness of the Gopis be Krishna, Every moment in my life Krishna,

Krishna in every corner of the world.

35

Everything lies in ShreeMati's feet....

अब सब तुम्हारी हाथ में है राधे,

मेरी जिंदगी यूं बंटी हुई है चिथडो में आधे।

मेरे हर खुशियों में राधे,

मेरे मन की पीड़ा हर लो माते ।

Meaning: -

Now everything is in your hands Radhe,

My life is divided into pieces like this. Radhe with all my happiness,

Mother, take away the pain of my mind.

36

The Story of Madhuban....

मधुबन की एक ये कहानी,

रस रचाये कृष्ण और राधे रानी।

गोपियों के मन यु हर्षाए,

गोकुल मे खुशियाँ है छाए।

Meaning :-

This is a story from Madhuban,

Krishna and Radhe Rani play rasa.

There is joy in the hearts of the Gopis,There is happiness in Gokul.

37

Meera's love for Krishna....

चौखट पे बैठी यूं वो मीरा,

यूं दिन और शाम बिताये.

कान्हा की यादों मे वो मीरा,

यूं झूम-झूम के गाए.

Meaning :-

That Mira, was sitting on the doorstep.Spent the day and evening.

That Mira in Kanha's memories,
Sang with joy.

38

When Kanha becomes your priority....

मेरे कान्हा, मेरे रक्षक,

मेरे कान्हा, मेरे शिक्षक।

मेरे कान्हा, मेरे हर इच्छा से हो कर,

मेरे कान्हा मेरे प्रणो से चढ़ कर।

Meaning :-

My Kanha, my protector,

My Kanha, my teacher.

My Kanha, makes my wishes true,My kanha is my everything.

39

His lotus feet....

हे कान्हा! ये तेरे सुंदर नयन,

करवा देते हैं मुझे गोकुल का चयन ।

और तेरे ये चरण ,

हे कान्हा! तू दे दे मुझे इन में शरण.

Meaning :-

Hey Kanha! These are your beautiful eyes,

Make me think about the Beauty of Gokul

And these lotus feet of yours,

Hey Kanha! May you give me shelter in these.

40

Damoodar....

दामोदर, अब तो किसी पर भरोसा भी नहीं होता।

क्योंकि इतना मेरा दिल टूट चूका है।

हे कान्हा! अब तो किसी से प्यार तक नहीं होता,

क्योंकि तुमसे मेरा दिल जो लग चुका है।

Meaning :-

Damodar, now I don't even trust anyone.

Because my heart is so broken.

Hey Kanha! Now I don't even want to love anyone,

Because my heart had already fallen in love with you.

41

Once upon a Meera & Radha....

यू मीरा घुट - घुट के गाती,

अपने मोहन के गुड़गान।

कान्हा तेरी बंसी,

पुकारे राधा का नाम.

Meaning :-

That Mira sing softly,

Gurgaan of her Mohan."Kanha, your flute, Call out Radha's name".

42

When Giridhar fills your life with colours....

गिरिधर ने रंग दिये खाली जिंदगी मेरी,

मेरे कान्हा ने यूं भर दी खाली उम्मीद मेरी।

Meaning :-

Giridhar gave colors to my empty life,

My Kanha has filled my empty hopes.

43

Radhey Rani....

वृन्दावन के गली - गली में बसी है राधे रानी,

दुनिया की यूं कण-कण में बसी है अपनी ठकुरानी.

Meaning: -

Radhe Rani resides in every nook and corner of Vrindavan.

Moreover our Thakurani is present in every corner of the world.

44

When I call, he always comes....

जब-जब मैंने उनको पुकारा,

तब-तब वो चले आए.

जब-जब मैंने उन्हें निहारा,

तब-तब वो मुसकुराए.

Meaning :-

Whenever I called him, He had always came. Whenever I looked at him, He smiled with his heart-melting smile .

45

Radhey Stays, Radhey heals....

अपने दयालु नयन बरसा दो मुझ पे राधे,

मेरी खाली फटी झोली भर दो राधे.

हर पल तेरा नाम रटूँ मैं,

मेरी ये पुकार सुन लो माते.

Meaning :-

Radhe, shower your kind eyes on me.

Radhe, fill my empty torn bag.

Every moment your name is in my heart,

Listen to my cry, mother.

46

His infinite love....

मैं कुछ ना भी बताऊँ उनको, तब भी मेरे कान्हा सब जानते है।

मैं कुछ छुपाऊँ भी ना, तब भी मेरे कान्हा सब देख लेते हैं।

Meaning :-

Even if I don't tell him anything, then also he knows everything.

Even if I hide something, then also my Kanha sees everything.

47

His smile....

हे कान्हा! तेरी मुस्कान तो मेरे दिल को पिघला देती है,

हे दामोदर! तेरी आंखें मेरी हर दर्द समझ लेती है।

Meaning :-

Hey Kanha! Your smile melts my heart,

Hey Damodar! You are the only one to understand my every pain.

48

When Krishna becomes your first and last priority....

कान्हा इस पूरी दुनिया में सबसे पहले मुसीबत में मेरा हाथ थामने वाले तुम ही थे,

हे कान्हा! यह पूरी दुनिया मे मेरे साथ देने वाले तुम ही थे।

Meaning :-

Kanha, you were the first one in this whole world to hold my hand in trouble.

Hey Kanha! You were the one in this whole world who supported me .

49

My tears are only wept by Kanha....

इस दुनिया को तो मेरे आंसुओं की कोई कीमत नहीं,

तो सोचा दामोदर के सामने थोड़े आंसू गिराने चाहिए।

फिर जब उनके दरबार में गई,

तो रोने से पहले ही लीला धर ने मेरे आंसू पोंछ दिये!

Meaning :-

My tears have no value to this world,

So I thought that I should shed a few tears in front of my Damodar.

Then,when I went to his court,

So Leeladhar wiped my tears before I could cry!

50

His beauty....

चलो आज मैं अपने कान्हा के बारे में बताती हूँ :-

मेरे कान्हा की आँखों में है प्रेम सागर से गहरा,

उनकी मुस्कुराहट में चाँद है पखेरा।

उनका तिलक किसी शान की शोभा से कम नहीं,

उनके फूल जैसे चरण किसी स्वर्ग से कम नहीं।

हे कान्हा! शायद मैं इन शब्दों से तुम्हारी सुन्दरता तो नाप नहीं सकती,

पर अंदाज़ा है कि कुछ ऐसे ही दिखते होगे तुम, जैसा मैं लिख सकती।

कान्हा मेरे शब्दों में तो बस इतना ही लिख सकती,

हे दामोदर! काश इस दुनिया पे गिरने की जगह तुम्हारे, चरण में यु गिर पड़ती!

Meaning :-

Let me tell you about my Kanha today:-

The love in my Kanha's eyes is deeper than the ocean,

The moon is shining in his smile.

His tilak is no less than a beauty of pride,

His flower like feet are no less than heaven.

Hey Kanha! Perhaps your beauty cannot be described in just wordS ,

But I guess that you look similar to which I had written.

Kanha, I can only write this much in my words,

Hey Damodar! I wish instead of falling on this world, I would have fallen onto your lotus feet!

Meera Bai

{Not a woman but the ocean full of love and devotion}

In the today's world we had probably heard this name 'Meera Bai' several times and most of us are knowing too. But the main thing to be focused is that she is not a simple woman, actually she is a Farishta (angle) who was send by Radhevallabh, to teach this fake world the menaing of true love and devotion. Her eyes were seeking love, her heart was pumping blood in which the blood cells were replaced by pure devotion, her smile teaches us that even in a pain, the rose bloom along with its thrones!

Radhey Radhey

www.ingramcontent.com/pod-product-compliance
Lightning Source LLC
LaVergne TN
LVHW041129150826
845673LV00007B/2243

9798894750989